Generational Success

Succession, Survival and New Leadership in Family-Owned Businesses

Chetan Walia

All rights reserved. No part of this
Publication may be reproduced, stored
in a retrieval system, or transmitted in
any form or by any means, electronic,
mechanical, photocopying or otherwise,
without the prior permission of the
copyright owner.

ISBN-13: 978-1720562849
ISBN-10: 1720562849

© ChetanWalia 2018 and BeOne Foundation For Transformational Leadership
www.thebeone.com

This white paper is presented by

BeOne Foundation For Transformational Leadership to contribute toward perpetuating the family businesses and their legacies so that they can have a continued impact on building economies, nations and the world.

Contents

	Executive Summary	7
1.	Introduction	8
2.	Taking A Global View: A Look at Family - Owned Businesses in the US, Germany, Jamaica, Saudi Arabia, United Arab Emirates and India	10
3.	A Comparison of Trends and Roles Inside Family-Owned Businesses	24
4.	A Look at Risk Failure and Success Stories in Family-Owned Businesses	32
5.	Innovation, Rejuvenation, and Longevity: New Practices for Family-Owned Business Success	40
6.	Conclusion	45

Executive Summary

The statistics are clear: family-owned businesses create and contribute a vast amount of wealth in local economies and around the globe; and yet their survival rates remain dismal and declining over successive generations. With such a powerful economic engine at stake, this white paper sets out to discover the causes of these failures or failures of succession. This paper's central concern is discovering new best practices in leadership and innovation to combat or prevent succession failure and ensure the longevity and continued economic impact of family-owned businesses.

Using in-depth industry research and analysis, the following sections will develop an overview of family-owned businesses—their various forms of operation, stories of inception, economic impact, trends, and risks; a global view of family-owned businesses, and their cultural practices, in different countries; anecdotal evidence of emerging innovations that have sustained and enlivened family-owned businesses and prevented succession failure; and ultimately to recommend the specific practices that business leaders should adopt or eschew. The overall hope is to teach and spread proven methods of leadership, problem-solving, succession planning, training, and innovation so that family-owned businesses remain intact, independent, and impactful.

1. Introduction

Family-owned businesses have historically generated a significant portion of GDP, and continue to make a large contribution to countries and global markets. Estimates on their actual economic impact range from families influencing between 35% and 45% of the United States' 500 largest companies, to contributing up to 64% of the United States GDP, to family-owned businesses providing employment to 60% of America's workforce, to a projection that by the year 2025, family-owned businesses will represent 40% of the world's largest enterprises.

A report in India suggests that family owned businesses account for 90% of its Gross Industry Output and for 79% of organized private sector employment.

It is no surprise, then, that family-owned businesses—their successes, struggles, unique traits, and even their failures—are of deep concern and remain a highly-researched topic in business, finance, and economics, with over 300,000 peer-reviewed journal and periodical articles just in the major databases. New entrepreneurs look to family-owned businesses for models of success, longevity, and wealth succession. Economists look to them to discern a pattern or strategy that can be adapted and disseminated, in order to increase success in other sectors.

Yet, the reality of family-owned businesses remains a mysterious blend of remarkable success, endurance, and mainstream notoriety, combined with a darker side of inheritance feuds, instability, and failure to survive past the third or fourth generation. The data on family-owned business succession varies as much as the data on their economic impact. Forbes claims that "less than one third of family businesses survive the transition from first to second generation ownership. Another 50% don't survive the transition from second to third." Entrepreneur puts the numbers even lower, at 30% surviving to the second generation, and only 12% surviving into the third.

Another research by a private consulting company claims that only 3% of family businesses survive into the fourth generation.

This white paper sets out to explore the inherent succession and

survival dilemma of family-owned businesses. Examining data, narratives, and overall historical trends, this paper will analyze the major causes of failure beyond the second generation of family-owned businesses; identify international examples of successes that defy the general failure rate; and ultimately, through determining areas of highest need and historically biggest impediments, discover the future's best business practices to ensure new and emerging family-owned businesses have the best chance for success, survival, and longevity.

2. Taking a Global View: A Look at Family-Owned Businesses in the US, Germany, Jamaica, Saudi Arabia, United Arab Emirates and India

Immigrant Family-Owned Businesses in the United States

In the United States, a typical family-owned business' origin story sounds something like this: an immigrant, usually recently arrived and without starting capital, uses his ethnic enclave's community resources and social support to start a small business. This business, hyper-local and small-scale, fills a pressing need in the area, filling a gap in an often difficult or time-consuming labor market. We see copious examples of ethnic groups establishing themselves as providers of much-needed services, often at lower costs than competitors, and often in less desirable locations.

In 1992, The New Yorker named this phenomenon the "immigrant job specialty," explaining that while "the forces that draw immigrant groups to certain occupations and businesses—Indians to gas stations, Koreans and Dominicans to grocery stores and Afghans to fried chicken places—are complex and varied. Their occupational choices are based on factors like skills and values learned in the old country, the paths followed by fellow immigrants who preceded them, or merely a lack of more attractive economic options."

"The common thread" the article's author, Donnatella Lorch, continues, "linking all immigrant work niches is the insider's edge on the profession. 'Recruiting through the ethnic network is the most efficient way the employer gets labor,' explained Roger Waldinger, a sociologist at UCLA who has studied and written extensively on Koreans and Dominicans in New York City. Ethnic labor, in particular family labor, is cheap and easily exploited and there is no linguistic, cultural or discriminatory barrier. Many immigrants are self-employed entrepreneurs."

Lessons from US Immigrant Family Businesses and Assimilation

Lorch's vivid description shows how countless family-owned businesses are created out of a constellation of needs, and sustained through blood ties, outsider culture, non-native language. While it is not the intent of this paper to focus solely on immigrant-owned businesses in the United States, these groups merit a particular analysis because of their sheer numbers as also because these are the very ethos of the first generation businesses that emerge in developing nations.

What immigrant family-owned businesses and start ups of yesteryears demonstrate is that **several pressing needs converge to create these businesses, some out of the entrepreneurs' volition and some out of their control entirely.**

Another noticeable characteristic is how these immigrant businesses alter the typical view of family immigration—not for the sake of maintaining closeness, but as a recruitment tool. This leads to a topic to be explored in a later section—how businesses often depend on the delicacy of family relations, and how a breakdown in familial relationships can risk the entire enterprise.

A complicated dilemma arises when cultural assimilation begins, usually in the first and second generation. When a business is founded on an outsider, subculture status, and maintained by deeply shared, private, family dynamics, the question arises of what happens when the once-cohesive network, culture, and business environment, is suddenly pierced by the dominant culture? **Furthermore, if a family-owned business is conceived and then sustained on outsider status, innovation can become too great a risk.**

In the next section, this paper will examine the culture of family-owned businesses in Germany, and explore the difference between American family-owned business outsider status, and Germany's political and social support of family-owned businesses.

Mittelstand: Class and Family-Owned Businesses in Germany

In Germany, a much smaller and more homogenous nation than the United

States, family-owned businesses are tied to class and socioeconomics, and subject to wider cultural approval and disapproval. German family-owned business history and practices serve as a stark contrast to the United States, in that Germany expects and maintains standard practices, ethics, and social obligations. Not surprisingly, German family-owned businesses do not suffer the same succession failure rate as do those in America.

According to an in-depth 2006 study by Hartmut Berghoff in *The Business History Review*, the German family-owned business is not simply an economic phenomenon or a function of capitalism. It is, in fact, a business sector all unto itself. In Germany, even "giant corporations such as Bertelsmann, Oetker, Henkel, Haniel, Metro, Bosch, BMW, Aldi, Lidl...are under family control, although most of these families have withdrawn from management" (Berghoff, 272). In addition, these particular businesses, which can range from the micro to employing over 1,000, German family-owned businesses belong to a social class called the "Mittelstand," characterized by its dedication to family-owned and operated companies in any industry.

"The term" writes Berghoff "refers to the 'middle rank' or 'golden middle,' something that strikes a balance between grinding poverty and immoral riches. Mittelstand to this day remains a very attractive social concept. To be part of the Mittelstand means to be generally acceptable as a person of solid and legitimate wealth" (Berghoff, 264).

The Mittelstand is not so much a direct translation of "middle class" as Americans would understand it. Rather, "Mittelstand" refers more to a mindset shared by family-owned businesses that values independence from cartels or associations; strong internal cohesion and mistrust of outsiders; consolidated management and control; generational continuity; emotional attachment to one's business and industry; careful training and apprenticeship; and not straying far from core competencies.

While family-owned businesses in other countries may earn a certain level of regard or even praise, in Germany, the Mittelstand enjoys wide social approval and political support. Germans *want* to be considered Mittelstand, considering it of honor and value to be deemed earners of their wealth rather than inheritors, and basking in the identity of a group that upholds strong work ethics and eschews elaborate and crass displays of wealth.

Does Stability and Social Support Mean Lack of Innovation?

All these Mittelstand characteristics, vastly different from family-owned business context in the United States, would seem to indicate a kind of rigidity that would stifle growth, expansion, or innovation. With the tightly controlled, regulated, and inherited system, one could assume little change from generation to generation. However, the story of Reinhold Wurth serves to dispel this assumption. In 1949, Wurth began apprenticing in his father's screw manufacturing and retail shop. At 19, he took over the business and expanded "the regional screw shop into a multi-national wholesaler of high-quality repair and assembly materials, ranging from plugs to construction fittings and stock-keeping systems." (Berghoff, 271).

Additionally, the well-established Daimler-Benz corporation has managed to vertically integrate itself with multiple suppliers. While foregoing small parts of its autonomy, they simultaneously "benefitted from the creation of a long-lasting alliance with a strong partner who made them work with other SMEs along the value chain" (Berghoff, 275). **The Mittelstand shows that a strong social standing, government support, and long-held practices do not hinder growth, expansion, or risk-taking.**

Family Values in Jamaican Family-Owned Businesses

A look at Jamaican family-owned businesses explores how the small nation's family values contribute to business resilience. Noel M. Cowell and Tanzia S. Saunders, in their 2010 article in *Social and Economic Studies,* use interviews and primary research to explore employment relations in family-owned businesses in Jamaica. They looked at all levels of family relationships: nuclear, immediate, and extended.

The authors' first finding was that family-owned businesses in Jamaica tended to be averse, even "generally hostile" to unionization and union organization. Rather than relying on a union structure, family-owned businesses relied on "paying well, maintaining a family atmosphere...and discipline" (Cowell and Saunders, 106). Family organization, with its unequally distributed and generationally-determined power structure, stands in contrast to outside union organization that put all employees on equal footing.

Second, in Jamaica, the family structure seems to have also superseded the standard corporate governance structure. All family-owned businesses examined by Cowell and Saunders "displayed an absence of formality in structures and procedures, fluidity in communication and decision-making, vague lines of demarcation, a lack of formal accountability framework, and a close alignment between family, ownership, and authority," all of which led to both "functional and dysfunctional outcomes." The authors write, "the hierarchy of the business was a reflection of the hierarchy of the family" (107).

And then there is the important dynamic of family members functioning as co-workers, who embody the values of the organization but are relied on to undertake critical tasks that demand loyalty, commitment, and trust (Cowell and Saunders, 110). On the downside of this tight-knit working environment is that "nepotism is institutionalized in family-owned businesses, particularly those that are small and recently formed…core family workers are unlikely to be removed from their positions and…are paid regardless of competence or value added contributions" (Cowell and Saunders, 111).

Other characteristics of Jamaican family-owned businesses included a lack of a formal board of directors; untitled roles arrived at by default or volunteer rather than deliberate hire; lack of formal, centralized authority; and no structured mechanism for compensation or accountability.

Lessons from Jamaican Family Dynamics

When the business model is shaped after the family model, a fascinating dynamic arises, and positive and negative practices take hold. Among the unfair practices that become entrenched are family members who enjoy unearned benefits of promotion and compensation. A business that includes employees who are both family and non-family members risks divisiveness and envy when family members are given priority and power, not because of their merits alone, but also because of their family position.

From the data, an important conclusion is that these family-owned business structures and successes are based on a deep level of trust

and unspoken expectations. Rather than rely on official policies and procedures, these families rely on informal communication and unspoken expectations.

New Wealth and Succession Planning in Saudi Arabia

In 2016, *The Economist* estimated that Saudi Arabia not only has higher rates of family-owned businesses that most other nations ("80% of the companies in the region, producing more than 90% of its non-oil wealth, are family owned"), but also higher than average rates of those business' failures, which the article's authors cite as up to 97% by the fourth generation.

In this oil-rich nation, made suddenly wealthy by recent land and oil booms, families have become overnight businesses of staggering size and capital. The resulting responsibilities have not always been easy to cope with, and one of the biggest dilemmas facing Saudi family-owned businesses is how to plan for succession. Several difficulties stem from the dominant cultural practices in Saudi Arabia, and some of them from the lack of instilling good governance practices.

For example, Saudi cultural practice gives the first-born son succession rights, regardless of his abilities or interest. When this doesn't function in the best interest of the business, the article notes the practice of "companies get[ting] around incompetent heads by creating parallel structures so that the real power is held by people with minor titles, or by avoiding naming a CEO at all." In contrast to the Jamaican family values infusing their business practices, this Saudi tradition is actually a hindrance to long-term business strategies.

Further, there is the problem of blurred lines between family and business money and power. "Too many," write the authors, of the region's businesses blur the line between what belongs to the firm and what belongs to the family: they spend company money as if it were their own and employ family members without subjecting them to proper vetting."

All of these difficulties are exacerbated by the very newness of the wealth and power. When a family hasn't planned for or built its own empire, but rather had it thrust into their possession by a sudden windfall or inheritance. Careful planning has to happen after the company and wealth is acquired, making the task doubly challenging.

Calls to change Saudi Arabia's family-owned businesses are coming most notably by the head of Crescent Enterprises, Badr Jafar. He tells *The Economist* that "regulators should compel companies to make clearer distinction between corporate property and family property." Most notably, he recommends that Saudi family businesses "should borrow mechanisms that are popular with family companies around the world—such as family constitutions, family meetings, and family offices—and adapt them to local traditions."

And some companies are hearing Mr. Jafar's calls. The rules are changing in several of Saudi Arabia's biggest family firms. Some have already begun to hold regular family gatherings to promote cohesion, or have required family employees to receive training and assessment. Other corporations have limited family roles to board membership or building separate office suites for family members, and are no longer sharing business and family resources. These changes seem just the beginning, as Saudi Arabia untangles itself from its deeply held family traditions, and begins to emerge as a business entity separate from the family unit.

Success Factors Linked to Sustainability of United Arab Emirates Family-Owned Businesses

The discussion now turns to a business sector in the United Arab Emirates, where family business accounts for 80% of non-oil and gas GDP and generate more than 70% of the employment in the region (Oudah, et. al. 246). Out of a need for one study to look comprehensively at a combination of success factors, authors Mohammed Oudah, Fauzia Jabeen, and Christopher Dixon "combine all success factors reported in the literature to help UAE based family businesses to sustain themselves across generations" (1).

The authors' 2018 study, published in *Sustainability,* is a crucial and timely examination, since "many of the medium and large sized family businesses are now in the first-and second-generation leading stage." Now is the time for the UAE to seek sustainable practices to help these businesses survive, most especially as **"an estimated one trillion dollars in assets are going to be transferred to the UAE's next generation of family businesses"** (3).

Using the World Commission on Environment and Development's definition, Oudah et. al. focus on *sustainability* as "meeting current needs without compromising the next generation's ability to meet its needs" (4). To complete their study, the authors combine that definition with the UAE business sector's definition of a *family business*: "a business in which at least 51% of the shares are owned by a single family and at least one member of the management team is chosen from the owning family" (3).

Finally, the authors bring together seven success factors from the existing literature, in order to examine them comprehensively. These seven criteria are the basis for the authors' new kind of study—putting these criteria together for the first time, to be examined together in light of how they contribute to a family-owned business' success or failure (7).

The seven success factors linked to the survival of the family business are:

1. **Succession Planning**

    - A structured approach to plan ahead for leadership positions in the family business.

    - Important to be established ahead of the death (sudden or foreseen) of the family business founder or leader.

    - Must be initiated by the founder, and continuously updated even after a successful business transition. (4)

2. **Strategic Planning**

    - Process of developing a business strategy for creating internal and external operations to establish profitable growth.

- Establishes a business' scope and long-term goals; adopts resources and competencies in changing environments.

- Different generational management stages will need different strategic and succession planning. (5)

3. **Corporate Governance**

    - Both the firm and family need structured governance to avoid conflicts that arise due to difficulty in separating family matters from business matters, and difficulty in decision-making, legacy, and leadership. (5)

4. **Leadership**

    - Guiding others to understand and accept what needs to be done and how it is to be done; the process of helping individuals equip themselves with knowledge to accomplish a unified objective.

    - The founder or incumbent leader must teach and train successors to lead with knowledge and skills necessary to continue the next generation of the business. (5)

5. **Family Business Values**

    - Configuring a common vision and creating a code of work; these are clear and desirable goals for both family and business life.

    - Clear and distinct values will help avoid conflicts of interest, streamline decision making, and assist in achieving larger goals.

    - Important values that highly contribute to firm longevity: quality, honesty, and hard work. (6)

6. **Family Capital**

- Represents the total resources of the owning family members; three components of family capital are: human, social, and financial capital.

- Limits to human capital must be seriously considered when assigning positions and roles.

- Networking and interactions among individuals and corporations that benefit the current and long-term business plans comprise social capital. (6)

7. **Family Firm Advisors**

- Comprised of *formal advisors* (accountants, lawyers, bankers, estate planners, therapists, etc.), *informal advisors* (mentors and associates), and *board members* (advisory or decision-making body for the firm's strategy, performance, succession and conflicts).

- Used to develop plans, answer questions, align goals, and resolve conflicts.

- Family and business advisors should be kept separate, and work toward the interests of their assigned body.

Using these seven criteria, Oudah et. al. proceed with their study to determine their influence on family firms' success. In a six-step process, the authors define the problem of sustaining multi-generation family businesses, develop a hierarchical structure of the problem, construct a pairwise comparison matrix, interview study participants, synthesize data, measure its consistency, and draw their conclusions.

The authors' findings show discrepancies between large and medium firms' attention and rating of the seven criteria, and they show the spread of all firms' ratings that highlight their strengths and vulnerabilities.

Large firms emphasized and rated succession planning and strategic planning highly. Large firms in turn rated family values as lowest, implying their family values are "weak or not well defined" (17), and rated family capital as second-to-last in importance, signifying "business resources and social network are already well established, and family members do not invest much time in building their human, social, and financial capital (17).

On the other hand, medium-sized firms rated corporate and family governance as low in priority, but rated leadership with the highest significance. Medium-sized firms put family capital second-highest, and family firm advisors as absolute lowest in their rankings.

The authors conclude their major findings:

> The major findings of this study are that large family businesses in the UAE are aware of transition failure and have long-term planning for their future generations in place; however they need to give more importance to abiding by family values and building the family capital. On the other hand, medium sized family businesses in the UAE are less aware of transition failure and have less long-term planning. Therefore, they need to create and give more importance to succession planning, strategic planning, and corporate governance to ensure their business longevity.

Understanding Family Business In India

According to the Credit Suisse Research Institute's (CSRI) latest "CS Family 1000" report, with an average market capitalisation of $6.5 billion, India ranks fifth in the Asia-Pacific excluding Japan, and 22nd globally, in terms of average m-cap for publicly listed family owned businesses.

In India the majority of businesses are in the dominant control of the families. It is estimated that 90% of the business in India is controlled by families. From 'Mom and Pop' Kirana stores to large conglomerates and SME's one finds family run businesses. Most of the big corporate business houses like Tatas, Ambanis, Birlas, Godrej, Wadias, Munjals, Mahindra, Thapars, Mittals, Shaparji Paollonji, Jindals, Adanis, Bajaj, Ruias, Ranbaxy, Times of India and many more are all controlled by families. The role of family and the family patriarch is quite important in India.

There are many families who have separated and partitioned. Some such families have succeeded and the separated branches have also grown big, while in some cases the branches which have separated or the business as a whole have failed or collapsed.

The Economic Liberalisation Of the 90s meant a large and growing number of new family groups have appeared on the corporate landscape in the 1990s. Many of these are jostling with the old guard for a leadership position.

A Business Today research paper suggests that the period prior to the 90s - **The licence-permit raj days** meant that once businesses had the all-important pieces of paper in place, they could sit back and sell in a market of shortages. Most companies didn't 'market.' They 'allocated.' The events of the 1990s shattered that cosy world for ever. The new generation needed different skills. They still need to have the patience to deal with politicians and bureaucrats; but they also have to listen to cranky consumers, uptight quality control managers, and volatile trade union leaders. To top it all, they need to have the charisma to raise money in the capital markets and debating skills to field, or deflect, questions from pesky journalists.

As it emerges post the 90s, an aritcle in Forbes cites poor succession planning, lack of trusted advisers, family conflict, different visions between generations, lack of financial education for children as some of the major reasons why 70 percent of the family-owned businesses fail or are sold before they are passed on to the second generation and almost 90 percent don't make it to the third generation. Great wealth is a privilege and without a sense of stewardship and obligation, many rich descendants fall prey to ennui and boredom, failing to safeguard the family wealth or treat the business with respect which leads into disintegration of many family businesses.

Unlike the German model where societal values seem to be the inherent driver or the Middle East model where business continuation is itself necessary for the family to have a standing, the Indian businesses seem to be lured more by personal wealth creation opportunities and social status which is a result of the wealth than of the societal contribuion.

Many families fail to nurture a sense of responsibility, history, and family values in the next generation, thereby neglecting family capital of the family business. Unqualified relatives mantle positions of power simply because they are members of the founding family, this also results in disintegration of family businesses. A private research firm's research into Asian family businesses has concluded that the majority of the Asian businesses fail because of the internal factors rather than the external. These internal factors include failure to plan for succession and family conflicts and the surprising fact is that these conflicts are predictable and yet unplanned for because the prime driver is not the business continuation but short-term wealth generation.

An Emerging Trend - The point to note is promoters' stake in businesses is in decline as they stay on the growth path, according to a Kotak Wealth Management report. Many are becoming more widely owned and professionally managed, or acquiring others to grow. The influx of foreign capital into India has meant that capital has become more accessible to the founders. The traditional and the modern businesses seem to have a preference to capitalize on their valuations and cash out rather than to solve the generational problem

Lessons from Indian Business Scenarios

In India there is a huge emotional connect in addition to the business aspirations. Families have established and running large businesses which are growing further. The commitment levels and the passion has been astounding. The Economic positioning and Business Success avaenues have ensured participation of the next generation in the existing businesses for further growth. However generational contiuity may not be a preferred characteristic of the milennial successor. That pattern hough still holds good for the SMEs and newer firms in the country.

Social Support or Social Withdrawal: A Determinant of Long-term Success

Examining family-owned businesses in the US, Germany, Jamaica, Saudi Arabia, UAE and India we see that the interaction between the business and the larger society and government plays a defining role in the business. While US immigrant-owned businesses withdraw from outside contact, German family-owned businesses enjoy a widely-held regard. This difference is a result of language barriers, outsider status, and constantly fluctuating immigrant populations in the US. And as a result, the immigrant-owned business in the US stay tightly closed to the outside, relying on family bonds, shared subculture, and non-English communication to survive.

In contrast, Jamaican family-owned businesses choose to separate themselves from the larger society's practices, especially from union organization. Their careful cultivation of family structures, dynamics, and hierarchy within the workplace gives these businesses more power, control, and freedom to run their businesses in a way that aligns with their family values. Meanwhile, Saudi Arabia's family-owned business can't seem to find enough separation between family and business, and UAE family firms are contending with disparate priorities that both help and hinder their succession and resolution plans.

In India and China, economy itself has driven businesses through Entrepreneurial ability and that seemingly sustains businesses through. The problem occurs when the future generations born into greater comfort and westernized education fail to grasp the nuances Indian societies.

Clearly, the level of autonomy and isolation a family-owned business perceives in itself has impacts in its business practices. When it therefore comes to succession, the business that sees a future for itself and actively plans for a new generation will have an advantage. For US immigrant-owned businesses, their outsider status can be hazardous to their successions. If they continue to operate in the shadows, depending only on family labor out of fear, their succession remains at risk. Similarly in an Indian scenario the struggle for remaining in power and control in the name of not having worthy successors itself becomes a reason for not having them. How can a family plan for its future without the possibility of opening up its business to the wider world?

On the other hand, businesses don't want to risk growing complacent with unspoken and unregulated family practices that never get codified into business practices. The important question remains: how can family-owned businesses receive the social support and regard of the Mittelstand, while exercising the freedom and independence of the Jamaican businesses? **How can family-owned businesses across the globe remain free and family-focused without having to sacrifice social ties and societal influence?**

3. A Comparison of Trends and Roles Inside Family-Owned Businesses

The literature on family-owned businesses tends to compare them to larger corporations not held or managed by related persons. To discover the particular factors that may contribute directly to family-owned business' ultimate successes or failures, this section will examine common practices, trends, and employee roles.

Conflict and Leadership Choices

According to a 2013 survey by Deloitte Development LLC, 28% of family-owned businesses do not use a board of directors. While that does mean that the majority of businesses do receive some kind of oversight from a board of directors, board of advisors, or family council, 43% of those report that their boards are comprised mostly of family members. Additionally, many of their non-family board members have some kind of business investment with the firm, creating a potential conflict of interest (McGee, 3).

According to the Canadian publication, *The Globe and Mail*, family-owned corporations should take the further step of establishing two different kinds of governance structures, with one specifically for family and one for other shareholders. "Family governance," writes Leah Golob, "requires family meetings, councils, or assemblies." Any family-owned business, Golob continues, risks "exclusion of family members outside the business."

The Risks of Informal Governance

The overall risks here are in the potential conflicts within the firm. When conflict arises, the risk of not having a formal governance structure are apparent. Who conflicting parties appeal to may not be codified; methods of resolving conflicts may not be wholly agreed upon; and procedures for grievance or appeals may not even exist. While informal structures may allow family-owned businesses to model their organizational charts and roles after the family structure, thereby maintaining trust and a close bond, the risks of conflict always loom.

Ethics and Trust

Wealth is typically considered in terms of capital, power, and influence. This seems true for non-family-owned businesses that make their primary aspirations increasing profits. Family-owned businesses, on the other hand, often set goals aside from and in addition to wealth accumulation. There are cases though where this itself becomes a conflict.

Socioemotional Wealth (SEW), and Corporate Misconduct

These alternative, non-economic goals, including "reputation and social identity," are, write authors Shujun Ding and Zhenyu Wu in *Journal of Business Ethics,* "an important dimension of SEW" (185). Ding and Wu's 2014 article uses Luis Gomez-Mejia, et al. definition of "socioemotional wealth" (SEW) as "the non-economic values that families derive from owning and controlling a business, and is believed to be the main driver of family firms' behavior" (Ding and Wu, 185).

The authors continue: "The pursuit of long-term growth and development by family firms makes trans-generational and intra-family succession an important issue. These are believed to be primary goals if firms are family owned" (Ding and Wu, 184). It shouldn't be surprising that a business grounded in familial relationships, all of which have their own dimension and importance, would want to focus on measures of success beyond profits. This seems especially true when family-owned businesses are well-established and have more to lose, likely when a founder is aging and concerned about succession: "When family-controlled firms are relatively mature, they grant priority to the preservation of SEW, including family legacy and dynasty, reputation, and so on" (Ding and Wu, 185).

In the same study, Ding and Wu compare the occurrences of ethical misconduct among family-owned and non-family-owned businesses. The results of their empirical study show that "small family firms are less likely to commit corporate misconduct than small non-family firms, and this mainly results from their intention for trans-generational succession of moral capital." Part of their findings stem from a family firm's age and maturity. **The correlation is clear: older family firms are more concerned with moral capital and less likely to commit corporate misconduct.**

The Ethical Climate

Mojca Duh, et. al, contribute to the study of ethics in their 2010 article, "Core Values, Culture, and Ethical Climate as Constitutional Elements of Ethical Behavior." Ethical behavior, the authors write, is "a precondition for an enterprise to obtain the status of a credible and trustworthy partner, which in the long-run ensures the enterprise's success" (473). Their article sets out to examine whether the ethical climate in family and non-family businesses differ, and how much this is influenced by family. Knowing that "an enterprise's positive attitude towards the ethical core values influences the emergence of the ethical climate necessary for the enterprises' ethical behavior," the authors track how much of this particular climate is created and maintained by family values.

What do the authors mean by "core values?" Essentially, "values serve to convey a sense of identity to its members, enhance the stability of its social system, direct managers' attention to important issues, guide subsequent decisions by managers, and facilitate commitment to something larger than self" (Duh, 475).

Taken from author Domingo Garcia-Marza (2005), the core ethical values are:

- Integrity
- Credibility
- Fairness
- Dialogue
- Transparency
- Dignity
- Legality
- Civic commitment
- Environment
- Responsibility

These ethical values "influence individuals' choices and lead to actions that every organization supports" (Duh, 276).

The authors cite a 1996 study that indicated "no significant differences exist regarding the types of ethical dilemmas encountered" between family and non-family businesses, but that employees in non-family-owned businesses were "more likely to report having a formal code of ethics than those in family-owned firms." To make sense of this data, Duh, et. al. suppose that the common family shared interests or perhaps the deliberate choice *against* a formal code in favor of a more family-centered culture. "Role modeling and the informal transmission of behavior norms" might also contribute to the lack of formal ethical codes in family-owned businesses (481).

As for their research results, Duh, et. al., provide three findings that are useful to this white paper study. First, the authors find that the majority of family enterprises, which are majority run on clan culture with more personal leadership and mentoring, have a positive attitude toward core values related to ethical content (484). They also find that, "as expected, family enterprises are more caring than non-family ones" and that family businesses have a slightly higher respect for law and professional standards than non-family businesses.

Family and Non-Family Employees: Three Kinds of Commitment

One organizational challenge within family-owned businesses is the dynamic between employees who are family members, and those who are not. Not all family-owned businesses employ a mix of team members, but this particular dynamic demands our attention because it is unique to family-owned businesses. One can imagine the kinds of conflicts that might arise from nepotism practices, group inclusion and exclusion of non-family employees, and the complex dynamics among teams made up of different numbers of each kind of employee.

Manuel Carlos Vallejo set out in a 2009 study to explore "the commitments of people who work in family firms and are not members of the owning family" (379). Vallejo asks if "these employees differ in their level of commitment compared to employees of non-family firms?" The resulting article, "The Effects of Commitment of Non-Family Employees of Family Firms from the Perspective of Stewardship Theory" reveals this important gap in the research.

Of the various kinds of commitment, Vallejo identifies three: affective, continuance, and normative. **Affective commitment** "refers to identification and emotional attachment to the organization"; **continuance commitment** "refers to commitment based on the employee's recognition of the costs associated with leaving the organization"; and **normative commitment** "refers to commitment based on a sense of obligation to the organization" (380). All three commitments give an employee different reasons to stay with an organization: wanting to stay out of fondness; needing to stay because of perceived higher costs, risks, and involvement of leaving; and an obligation to stay out of internalized loyalty, family, or cultural pressures (380-81).

Vallejo's conclusions are multiple. Foremost, he finds a link between generational success and employee commitment and dedication. If the business survives through multiple generations, its success provides "a source of pride and satisfaction among its members" (386). This leaves business leaders in a bit of a quandary, in the form of a chicken-and-egg dilemma: **do family firms earn loyalty through business success, or does business success occur because of more employee loyalty?**

Perhaps his most intriguing finding demonstrates the strength of the family members' attitudes and feelings to influence the overall success of the business. When there is "attachment and fondness" demonstrated by the owning family for its own legacy, "this feeling is transmitted to the non-family employees almost certainly through the latent values in the firm's organizational culture" (387). Neither rules nor formal power structures have as much influence as the simple feelings of the owning family members.

Finally, Vallejo demonstrates that family firms may enjoy an advantage over non-family firms "because of the positive influence of identification on profitability, and involvement and identification on continuity, in family firms" (387). **All that loyalty and positive regard turns into better business results.**

"Inter-role Conflict" in Family-Owned Businesses

Since the literature so overwhelmingly focused on the problems of running and maintaining family-owned businesses, authors Terry A. Beehr, John Drexler, and Sonja Faulkner conducted a wide-ranging study on the kinds and levels of conflicts within family-owned firms, in order to discover specific advantages and disadvantages for the employees and the overall business. Their results are published in the *Journal of Organizational Behavior*.

Beehr, et. al, begin by confining their study to behavior-based conflicts, within the larger category of inter-role conflicts (which are "conflicts between demands from people whom the employee interacts on the basis of two different roles"). The authors emphasize that there are certainly advantages, many proven in the literature, to working in a firm owned by one's own family (299), even though they suggest that conflicts within family businesses "are likely to have more serious consequences than conflicts occurring in non-family businesses" (300).

Of their conclusions, the one most interesting for this paper is that working among family members was no more likely to cause conflict or serious problems (309). Another comparison result that stands out is the finding that non-family employees reported lower personal advantage than employees at non-family businesses, suggesting that **family-owned businesses are not always the most hospitable environments for non-family employees**. The authors offer this interpretation: "the advantages provided to family members, e.g. rapid advancement and increased responsibility, might translate into disadvantages for the non-family members" (309).

Overall, family members in Beehr's study reported feeling "more satisfied with their careers, more committed to the organization, and were perhaps somewhat less likely to quit than others" (310). These reports were not accompanied by *less* satisfaction or commitment from non-family employees, as one might expect.

Conflict is not something any business can maintain control over, like governance structure. But it is something that all firms must plan for, family-owned ones especially. With the unique and often delicate balance that must be maintained between family and non-family employees, these businesses must be wary of the effects of nepotism and the perception of non-family employees when family members get promotions, advancements, or other bonuses not equally distributed among all employees. **Most importantly, we can take from Beehr's findings that the structure of the family-owned business itself does not directly cause or exacerbate conflict. Owners must simply be much more cognizant of and careful with conflicts when they arise.**

CEO Satisfaction and Firm Performance

While many studies throughout the 1990s have examined how a firm's leadership affects its level of success, Catherine M. Daily and Janet P. Near examine a more particular characteristic: CEO life satisfaction. Many studies have been conducted to demonstrate the link between a CEO's psychology, origin, attitudes, and founding status, but this study from 1999 was the first to look at how a CEO's job satisfaction affects employee performance. "In a small, family business, in particular, the owner/manager is simply too important for attitudes not to affect employees' views and, presumably, firm performance overall" (Daily and Near, 130).

Previous CEO research indicates that self-employed individuals experience higher job and life satisfaction (Daily and Near, 139), and so the authors take this evidence and put it toward examining how job and life satisfaction of CEOs of family-owned businesses affect employees. The authors note that "owners/managers of small and/or family firms are likely to experience higher levels of job and life satisfaction than is the case for the average American worker," basing their claim on copious anecdotal evidence. Further, the authors concluded that "family business owners/managers found the job to influence their lives intensely," but that, in the end, a CEO's job satisfaction did not have a directly measurable impact on the firm's success, which was measured in productivity, sales, and growth.

Lessons from Comparing Family and Non-Family Enterprises

What is gained by comparing the practices and trends among family-owned and non-family businesses? What can businesses learn by studying the differences?

It's clear that different practices are necessary for different kinds of businesses, and that family-owned businesses thrive with certain practices that would certainly doom a traditional corporation. One cannot expect these two types of enterprises to function identically. However, even within this need for adaptation to family structures, we see that straying from traditional leadership hierarchies and procedures opens family-owned businesses to risks—largely contingent ones. Not having many formal structures in place create problems when conflict arises, but the lack itself does not seem to create the conflict.

And yet, from Manuel Carlos Vallejo, we see the benefits of unspoken family dynamics in the workplace. Namely the transmittal and transference of loyalty and investment in family legacy and business success, simply through the family members themselves holding a positive regard for the quality of their products and services.

The research is revealing: so much of what makes a family-owned business succeed or fail is unwritten, informal, and unstructured. So much of a business' longevity is based on intangible feelings, relationships, style, trust, and tradition.

In the next section, this paper will examine various anecdotes of successes and failures, to create a general picture of what concrete practices family-owned businesses can adopt or avoid.

4. A Look at Failure Risk and Success Stories in Family-Owned Businesses

We begin this section with an overview of critical mistakes documented and generalized by various sources, to try and come up with a broad analysis of what causes family-owned businesses to fail overall and fail in succession.

The Most Common Pitfalls that Lead to Dissolution or Succession Failure

In the USA Today article, "All in the Family," Brian Greenberg writes that "simply knowing how to navigate and circumvent personal relationships in order to work together effectively, while also maintaining positive perceptions and overall integrity" is key to a multi-generational business thriving. Simply knowing how to interact can save a family business.

Greenberg's list of pitfalls (72-73), which often lead to the death of a business include:

> *Not respecting family hierarchy.* The family structure naturally carries over to the business order, as do family roles, dynamics, responsibilities, and groupings. Greenberg advises against keeping family and business entirely separate. Trying to do so denies the unique nature of the arrangement and stifles family strengths.

> *Neglecting to define or agree upon roles.* Family members who do not actively help define their roles can get stuck in their old roles and be unable to move forward or grow. When roles are not made official with titles and responsibilities, everyone can lose their momentum.

> *Not allowing enough leeway.* Trying to treat family members exactly like non-family employees is simply denying reality, and can end up denying the family members' deep loyalties and commitments. This is especially true with younger members, who need to be given freedom and independence to lead their own projects, perhaps more leeway than a non-family employee would be given at that stage.

Not including the entire family on important decisions. Now that multiple generations can be involved in running the business, it can no longer be left only to the oldest generation to make decisions. Every family member has an investment, a unique perspective, and a deep commitment to success. Likewise, it's unwise to leave older members out of decisions, even if the reason is trying to spare them stress or trouble. Ageism, as well as in-law "outsider" status, can result in damaging conflict from members not feeling equally valued.

Not having a conflict resolution plan. When conflicts arise, they can often damage a business in unforeseen ways. Family businesses don't need completely formalized structures, but rather a simple plan that all parties agree upon, as to who has mediation or arbitration power. This will help avoid major consequences like litigation and resignations, but also the seemingly minor resentments that can upend a whole business' dynamics.

3 Most Common Traps That Can Destroy Family Businesses

George Stalk and Henry Foley explore more reasons why family-owned businesses fail or fail to endure, in their 2012 article, "Avoid the Traps that Can Destroy Family Businesses," published in Harvard Business Review. Part of the reason, they argue, is an inability to adapt to shifts and advances in technologies, and relying too much on the original method that the founder created.

The authors' three major traps include the following:

Treating the family business as a fallback. In the interest of fostering their children's independence, many business owners choose not to groom them for succession. While this is a generous position, it also creates a situation in which the offspring are made to feel that there will always be employment and opportunity in the family business, if other options fail. A guaranteed job, Stalk and Foley argue, is not good for character or organization morale.

The family grows faster than the business. Within a generation, a family can grow exponentially, thereby outgrowing the business itself. This may leave some family members without roles to play in the business, or with needs that the business revenue cannot meet. Business growth can be carefully planned, charted, contained, and stabilized. Family growth can't be so easily managed.

Maintaining isolated family and business roles. Often, fathers and sons maintain one set of roles, while mothers and daughters maintain another. This isolation can result in the subsequent generation "failing to gain cross-functional expertise needed for executive leadership." Along with family dynamics interfering with supervision and feedback, this can lead to what the authors call a "leadership vacuum" in the next generation.

No one act or omission causes a family-owned business to fail. Among the numerous countries, contexts, constraints, and cultural expectations, any one business' failure can likely be attributed to multiple causes. These critical mistakes highlight what to consciously avoid and deliberately plan for, in order to ensure a better chance at longevity and survival.

In the next section, two particular business insights give anecdotal cases for how inventive thinking can launch or save a family-owned business.

Success Story: The Mars Family Business' 4th Generation Endurance

This section is an in-depth overview of Mars, Inc., an American candy and pet food company founded by in 1911, and now headed by Victoria Mars. Ms. Mars is the the 4th generation family leader of the company, and now serves as Board Chairwoman.

In an interview with the Yale School of Management, Ms. Mars offers her direct experience and insights into why her family's business not only survived, but expanded and succeeded against the odds. "At Mars, Inc." she states, our objective is to create growth we're proud of. As an organization, we need to grow; and if you don't continue to grow, you die. So, growing is important."

Mars Inc. Succeeds with a Five Principles Foundation

Ms. Mars cites company culture, which is based on Five Principles, as the primary reason for the business' success. She calls these principles, that were made official in the 1980s, "family values" thereby emphasizing the original nature of the business, and the reliance on family structures and expectations to run a huge business. Ms. Mars underscores their importance:

> These are principles that we expect every one of our associates to live by. And it's not just about knowing what they are: it's actually making decisions in line with the principles. They're not just pretty words on a wall. The Five Principles are the foundation of how we do business—not the *what* of our business, but the *how* of our business.

Whether you call them a code of ethics or a set of rules, the Mars' Five Principles have sustained the corporation for over 100 years. Of course, each company will need to find its own set of guiding principles, and make them solid and enduring.

An Open and Fluid Company Culture

Additionally, Ms. Mars states that their organization's culture is based on "open communication and dialogue and idea-sharing." They achieve this by crafting a very open workspace and organizational chart. "We sit in open offices; nobody has a special private office. Everybody sits in open space; there are no walls, there are no doors, there are no secretaries to get past to see someone."

Ms. Mars acknowledges that this kind of structure certainly doesn't work for everyone. "I think every organization has a culture and every organization has a way of doing business, and I don't think every place is right for everybody."

But at Mars, Inc., equality is emphasized with staff integration and interaction. "We have hierarchy," Ms. Mars explains, "because every organization has hierarchy, but we minimize the impact of that hierarchy.

Whatever level you are in the organization, you can talk to anybody at any level. So, there's nothing that says, 'If you're this level you can't talk to the CEO or you can't talk to a vice president.'"

A Culture of Collaboration

In keeping with Mars Inc.'s open communication and flattened hierarchy, Ms. Mars also describes how the company collaborates on its direction and vision. When it's time to develop the company mission and goals, the decisions are not made at the top and then distributed. Instead, employees at Mars Inc., "develop the mission and goals together." Ms. Mars describes the process:

> It's not somebody sitting in a room and saying, 'Okay, well this is going to be our mission. Here you go; everybody take it.' It's a collaborative effort of people working together and that resonates with people. And then it's about communication and talking about it and making sure it's not just some words that somebody saw in a PowerPoint presentation or something that people bring out when they want to show something off.

What are the Disadvantages of Being a Family-Owned Company?

When asked the pointed question of whether there are any disadvantages to being a family-owned business, Ms. Mars stated, candidly, that while there are special needs that must be attended to, there are no special disadvantages to running her own company. "I don't think that's a disadvantage; it's just an added perspective that doesn't exist in a public business."

Ms. Mars elaborates further:

> The thing that is different in a private company is the need to find ways to keep the family engaged. You need to find a way to keep the family connected and educated about the business from generation to generation. You need policies that help govern the family as an entity connected to the company, which in a public business you don't have to do. However, being private, you retain the freedom to do what you think is the right thing, the right way, how you can make a positive impact while doing business.

Lessons from Mars Inc.

There are many valuable insights business leaders can glean from the values, principles, and practices at Mars Inc.

First, careful front-end planning is key to long-term success. The Mars Five Principles have been the cornerstone of their business for nearly 40 years, and help guide everything from hiring to meeting structures. Making up rules and changing them hastily or at the last minute are not conducive to strong, predictable, and foundational business practices.

Second, collaboration is crucial. Not many companies would be willing to collaborate at all levels about the mission of the firm as a whole. Yet, what better way to obtain employee buy-in and deep commitment? Mars Inc. runs its major, multi-national corporation like a small family business.

In a seemingly counter-intuitive move, Mars Inc. prioritizes company values and human resources beyond profits, and yet enjoys booming growth, expansion, and indeed profits. Though not in keeping with the corporate norms, Mars Inc. is defying the odds of family-owned business rates of succession failure, allowing them to outlast and outshine competition, and expand profits while maintaining integrity and fidelity to the founder.

Success Stories: Lasting Asian-American Entrepreneurship in the US

Moving into a more generalized group of successful family business owners, authors Alicia M. Robb and Robert W. Fairlie examine the success factors in Asian-owned businesses in the US, publishing their findings in a 2009 *Journal of Popular Economics* article.

Looking at the field research that indicates Asian-Owned business are "more likely to survive and are more profitable that businesses owned by other racial groups," the authors set out to examine what specific factors contribute to this group's success.

At the time of writing, the authors cite estimates from the Current Population Survey, that indicate Asians in the US have an 11% self-employment rate, higher than rates for other minority ethnic groups, and nearly equal to self-employment rates for white Americans. Asian-owned firms are additionally larger, more profitable, and have higher survival rates than white-owned firms. They are, according to CBO estimates, 16.9% less likely to close than white-owned businesses (830).

What could be the factors contributing to this group's success and longevity? Certainly, the literature has covered many: ethnic enclaves that transmit social and ethnic resources; high levels of human and financial capital; rotating credit associations; and access to co-ethnic labor and customers (831).

Using CBO data, the authors were able to examine four major business outcomes: closure, profits, employment, and sales (832). Some **general trends** discussed include:

- Small business outcomes are positively associated with the education level of the business owner (better business outcomes with each higher level of education).

- Urban businesses are more likely to have large profits and higher sales, but have a higher chance of closing and are less likely to have employees.

- Positive outcomes are associated with a family business background and apprentice-type training, level of management experience, amount of capital used at start-up.

- Marriage is associated with business success. (840)

- Inherited businesses are more successful than non-inherited ones. (835-37)

When making comparisons among Asian-owned businesses and those owned by whites or other minorities, the authors' **comparison findings** are in keeping with their trends:

- 46% of Asian business owners have at least a college degree (22% of those have gone beyond an undergraduate degree) compared with 33% of whites who have at least a college degree.

- 82% of Asian owners are married, compared with 77% of white married owners. (840)

- 13.8% of Asians used a personal loan from a family member for start-up capital, as opposed to 5.8% of whites. (841)

- Fewer than 47% of Asian-owned firms have an outstanding loan, compared with 56% of white-owned firms. (842)

- Asians start with more capital: 12% of Asian-owned firm started with more than $100,000 in capital, compared to 5% of white-owned firms. (843-44)

- 22% of Asian owners work 60+ hours per week, compared with 14% of white owners. (845)

In their conclusions, the authors state that amount of start-up capital and level of owner education are the two biggest determining factors of success, and the widest discrepancies between Asian-owned businesses and others. Several other factors, like region and industry, do not indicate a substantial link to business success. And number of hours worked by the owner is not strictly indicative of business success.

Overall, the lessons and insights gained from this data-driven comparison indicate that family-owned businesses would benefit from examining the level of education of their founder, and increasing their amount of start-up capital to try and ensure longevity and success.

5. Innovation, Rejuvenation, and Longevity: New Practices for Family-Owned Business Success

The picture for family-owned businesses is not entirely certain, but there are clear findings and conclusions that the previous sections draw: family businesses must consider succession planning, they must take care in how they are founded and by whom, and they must comport with certain governance structures and formalities. As seen previously, family-owned businesses that eschew formal structures fall victim to conflicts and succession failures. Family firms that do not codify, separate, and nurture family rules and business rules are less likely to survive.

The Missing Link in Family Business Success: Innovation and Entrepreneurial Vision for Lasting Renewal and Success

In all of these studies, planning for the future is the most important criteria connected to business longevity and family harmony. And yet, an important question remains: **what is the role of innovation in the future, success, longevity, and growth of family-owned businesses?** Indeed, an in-depth McKinsey & Co study states that "The classic family enterprise starts with an innovative founder who leads it through some of its most dramatic growth years. It's increasingly evident that maintaining this entrepreneurial edge is critical for long-term survival."

Yet, rarely are there studies or research on the topic of innovation, as it can be nebulous, changing, and subjective. However, most of the research, including that which appears in this paper, doesn't venture to speculate about this ineffable and risky skill might play a part in business success. The McKinsey & Co report continues: "it is difficult to parse the DNA of family businesses—a complex mix of family, management, and wealth creation, all overlaid with a rolling ownership dynamic that claims all but 30 percent of them by the third generation."

Of the four dimensions the McKinsey & Co analyze, three have already been covered in this paper (family capital, governance, and succession planning), but a fourth one sparks new interest, and covers completely new ground: **entrepreneurial vision.** After all, "renewal," the McKinsey & Co authors state, "is a strategic imperative." How, businesses must ask themselves, do they battle the "barriers to entrepreneurship and innovation [that] creep in?"

For starters, family businesses are exceedingly careful with their capital and are disinclined to take risks. McKinsey & Co reports that survey respondents described their companies' approach to innovation "as neutral rather than weak or strong." This attitude, however, "may not be as well suited to an era of profit constraints, when advantage is shifting to nimble, idea-intensive sectors." When family owners are more likely to avoid risks, "the result is often a failure of renewal and resolve."

How, then, does a family firm maintain or recover their entrepreneurial energy and innovation? McKinsey & Co finds that they can take three approaches:

1. **Align on an ownership strategy.** What this means is that while different family members will embrace different objectives, risk tolerances, and wealth preservation tendencies, owners must be aligned on "one set of objectives and guidelines" in order to "reduce the tensions that plague all multigenerational family businesses."

2. **Internalize the market's creative destruction**. It might benefit a family firm to divide its portfolio into three parts: Creation; Core; and Trading. Each part represents different activities, risks, and rules. This separation encourages diversity of managers and cultures, and forces the family firm to "build, operate, and terminate businesses constantly."

3. **Next-generation emotional ownership.** The next generation of family business owners overwhelmingly feel part of the family business, regardless of whether they work for it directly. Matching this next generation of talent with those components of a dynamic portfolio can diversify talent, encourage the young to pursue and master their passions, and let next-generation leaders "play a critical role in making this strategic pivot when they get the responsibility for bringing expertise" in different areas.

A Secret Formula for Success?

"Successful families," writes Joachim Schwass of the IMD Global Family

Business Center, "understand that they need to add value to the business, instead of just seeing the business as a provider of dividends. This added value on the part of family members comes in different shapes and forms, including actively leading the business, supporting the business strategies, understanding the business and industry deeply, playing ambassadorial roles, and, last but not least, caring for the communities in which the families' businesses operate" (Schwass, 9).

In his research analysis, "Family Businesses: Successes and Failures," Schwass provides an flow chart that aims at the sweet spot of family business success:

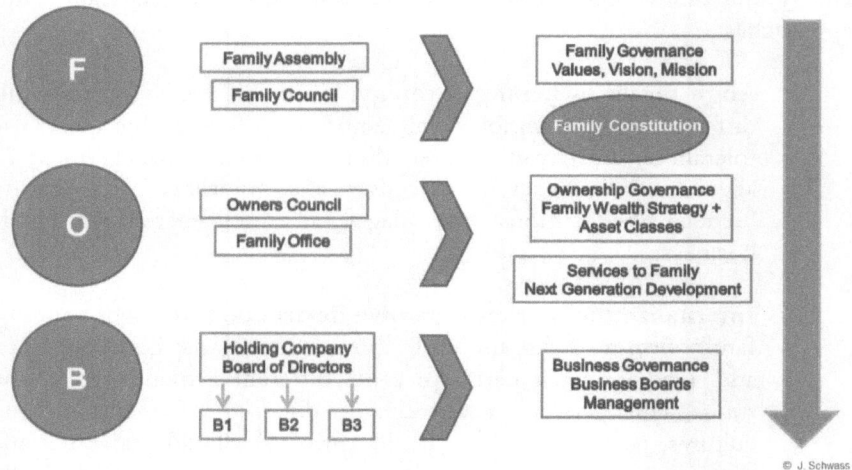

With a careful combination leadership, governance, management, and succession training, Schwass gives us a set of interrelated practices to set family businesses up for success.

The Next Generation: An Emotional and Identity Succession Planning

Moreover, in terms of power sharing and succession, we see a distinction between generations. Schwass states that the "I" generation and the "us" culture are sometimes at odds, pitting the dominant entrepreneur whose risks and revolutionary ways founded the business, against the "us" inheritors of multiple siblings or even cousins. "The *I generation* has never experienced a succession towards an *us culture*. This leaves the sibling generation typically ill prepared and lacking an effective role model." Founders, Schwass reminds us, "find it very difficult to let go of control and imagine the business without their leadership" (7). **In this new take on succession planning, Schwass is urging family businesses to plan for succession not just in terms of finances, power, governance, or growth, but in terms of emotion, vision, and self-determined identity.**

In another fresh take, Schwass looks at the family unit's responsibility for defining itself and its purposes. "Like a nation, the growing family needs to define WHY they want to stay together, HOW they are going to create decision-making structures, and finally WHO is going to exercise leadership." And when, as inevitably will happen, some family members are unwilling or unable to move forward with the business' growth, direction, or values, Schwass maintains that "successful families understand and accept this and facilitate their departure without unnecessarily 'punishing' them for their different views" (7).

Those who are left are faced with a new dilemma and opportunity—to determine their future together. After succession, and after the new leadership has been pared down to the remaining members, "those staying will feel stronger and more united as they define their shared vision or 'dream' for their own generation."

A Fearless Way Forward with Innovation and Succession

Austrian economist Joseph A. Shumpeter, often called "the father of entrepreneurship," gives perhaps to most enduring and succinct take on this paper's topic. In Sigurd Pacher's overview of Schumpeter's life and work, we see the economist's deepest held beliefs about "the role entrepreneurs play in breaking up old structures and creating new ones":

> Entrepreneurs, in his view, are the only ones who bring about long-term economic growth. They are not the "risk bearers," but the ones who continuously seek an innovative edge. Innovation drives progress and is itself driven by competition. It throws out the old and brings in the new. It unsettles the established order and brings with it turmoil... **[Schumpeter] insisted that without innovation**

> **there was no economic development and no wealth creation.** (Pacher).

What happens next, however, seems the opposite of Schumpeter's vision for the economy:

> ...large firms—both the source and the result of successful innovation—start to dominate economic life. Over time, they become more bureaucratic and tend to constrain innovation which morphs into a matter of routine (Pacher).

Family businesses must maintain the spirit of the entrepreneur, the risk, the innovation, and the rejuvenation, without descending into an entity that constrains rather than enlivens innovation.

By examining the international practices of family-owned businesses, warnings against failure, successes despite the odds, and paths forward through innovation, our conclusions rest on seeing growth as renewal and innovation, not just expansion and higher profits.

When family-owned businesses look at their visions of success, they must see risk, regeneration, and innovative edge. If the focus remains too much on who is in power to direct the company; if there is infighting between family and non-family employees; and if there are no standards for conflict management and forward movement, the family-owned business seems doomed to be yet another statistic.

But, if all generations and stakeholders of a family-owned business can create a stable and inclusive hierarchy, rely on insider and outsider advisors, see succession in terms of generational value shifts, and above all maintain an entrepreneurial spirit, there may indeed remain a chance for true defying-the-odds survival, endurance, and longevity.

6. Conclusion

The picture for family-owned businesses is not entirely certain, but there are clear findings and conclusions that the previous sections draw: family businesses must consider succession planning, they must take care in how they are founded and by whom, and they must comport with certain governance structures and formalities. As seen previously, family-owned businesses that eschew formal structures fall victim to conflicts and succession failures.

No matter how a family-owned business is born, whether out of need, an economic turn, an immigration, or a burning entrepreneurial spirit, the fact remains that our global economy cannot function without them. They have become an integral part of almost every nation's economic engine, contributing employment opportunities, needed services, and national GDP. We cannot underestimate the value of family-owned businesses, especially the small-to-medium sized firms.

In light of their alarming failure rates, it is incumbent upon the global business community to examine the literature and find new solutions. The literature reveals the many current and lurking problems family-owned business face, and the various ways leaders and employees can work to prevent or combat succession failure. In short, we know what's wrong and we know some concrete ways to avoid the failures of these vital economic engines. But, what is the way forward with this knowledge?

Clearly, family-owned businesses need solid succession planning, and now the way forward lies with a renewed kind of succession planning. When businesses look beyond profits and into their legacies, **they can see the value of emotions, vision, and the intangible entrepreneurial spirit they should strive to pass to the next generation.** There is no singular way to run a family business, or to ensure its survival. But there is **innovation**, which is an ideal, method, mindset, approach, and commitment that can steer a family and its business toward success and endurance, if it is followed wholly and fearlessly.

Works Cited

Aileron. "The Facts of Family Business." *Forbes.* 31 July 2013.

Baker, Daniel. "Many Family Businesses Struggle to Survive Past the Second Generation." *Black Enterprise.* 28 August 2013.

Beehr, Terry A. et al. "Working in Small Family Businesses: Empirical Comparisons to Non-Family Businesses." *Journal of Organizational Behavior*, vol. 18, no. 3, 1997, pp. 297–312. *JSTOR*, JSTOR,

Berghoff, Hartmut. "The End of Family Business? The Mittelstand and German Capitalism in Transition, 1949-2000." *The Business History Review*, vol. 80, no. 2, 2006, pp. 263–295. *JSTOR*, JSTOR,

Bjornberg, Asa, Ana Karina Dias, and Heinz-Peter Elstrodt. "Fine-tuning Family Business for a New Era." McKinsey & Company Organization. October 2016.

Bluestein, Adam. "The Most Entrepreneurial Group in America Wasn't Born in America." *Inc* 12 January 2015.

Card, Jon. "Secrets to Business Survival: Always Look at New Ways to Innovate. *The Guardian.* 15 March 2017.

Cowell, Noel M., and Tanzia S. Saunders. "Family Values and Employment Relations: A Jamaican Case Study." *Social and Economic Studies*, vol. 59, no. 3, 2010, pp. 97–126. *JSTOR*, JSTOR,

Daily, Catherine M., and Janet P. Near. "CEO Satisfaction and Firm Performance in Family Firms: Divergence between Theory and Practice." *Social Indicators Research*, vol. 51, no. 2, 2000, pp. 125–170. *JSTOR*, JSTOR,

Ding, Shujun, and Zhenyu Wu. "Family Ownership and Corporate Misconduct in U.S. Small Firms." *Journal of Business Ethics*, vol. 123, no. 2, 2014, pp. 183–195.,

Duh, Mojca, et al. "Core Values, Culture and Ethical Climate as

Constitutional Elements of Ethical Behaviour: Exploring Differences Between Family and Non-Family Enterprises." *Journal of Business Ethics*, vol. 97, no. 3, 2010, pp. 473–489. *JSTOR*, JSTOR,

Golob, Leah. "Ten Reasons Why Family Businesses Fail." *The Globe and Mail*. 20 July 2012. Updated 3 March 2018.

Lee, Yoon G. "Business Longevity and Dissolution: A Study of Family-Owned Businesses in the US" Conference Proceedings of the 6th Conference of the Asian Consumer and Family Economics Association.

Mars, Victoria. "How Does a Family Business Survive?" Yale Insights. Yale School of Management. 19 April 2017.

McGee, Tom. "Perspectives on Family-Owned Businesses: Governance and Succession Planning." Deloitte Development, LLC.

Oudah, Mohammed, et. al. "Determinants Linked to Family Business Sustainability in the UAE: An AHP Approach." *Sustainability*. 18 January 2018.

Pacher, Sigurd. "Innovation and Entrepreneurship-the Austrian Economist Joseph A. Schumpeter." Austrian Embassy Washington. 2014.

Robb, Alicia M., and Robert W. Fairlie. "Determinants of Business Success: An Examination of Asian-Owned Businesses in the USA." *Journal of Population Economics*, vol. 22, no. 4, 2009, pp. 827 858. *JSTOR*, JSTOR,

Schumpeter Columnist. "Succession Failure." *The Economist*. 4 February 2016.

Schwass, Joachim. "Family Businesses: Successes and Failures." IMD Global Family Business Center. International Institute for Management Development. 2013.

Scouler, Dan. "The Frequently Fatal Family Business Flaw: Denial." *Entrepreneur*. 25 Feb 2014.

Stalk, George Jr. and Henry Foley. "Avoid the Traps that Can Destroy Family Businesses." Harvard Business Review. January-February 2012.

The Economist. "Passing on the Crown." *The Economist Group Limited.* 4 Nov 2004.

Tohidi, Hamid and Mohammad Mehdi Jabbari. "The Importance of Innovation and its Crucial Role in Growth, Survival, and Success in Organizations." *Procedia Technology* Vol. 1. 2012.

Ward, John L. "The Special Role of Strategic Planning for Family Business." *Family Business Review* Vol 1 No. 2, 1988.